Ivanka Tr~~~~ ~ ~~~~~~~~

Ivanka Trump isn't necessarily a household name... anything mentioned about Trump and people automatically think of Donald. It wasn't until I started researching recently that I really even knew that Ivanka Trump was Donald Trump's eldest daughter and not his current wife (for anyone else struggling with the confusion, Melania is the current wife; Ivana, no "k", is the first ex-wife). This bio isn't about Donald and his love life... though I'm pretty sure many would find it easier to fill up a book on that than on the daughter of one of the most successful businessmen of all time. However, Ivanka Trump has certainly made her mark on the world, and she did it in the best way she knew how-- through business. She has learned how to promote herself and has done it well. From what I can tell, she could fill an entire department store with the stuff that is under her name and guidance. Anything from kids' shoes to handbags, from glasses to jewelry, she's designed it all. She even has her own lifestyle website!

Ivanka Trump is a driven woman, but that didn't come about overnight; she was raised that way. Her parents, Donald and Ivana, raised her and her two brothers, Don Jr. and Eric, to fight for what they want and to win no matter what. There are stories that Ivanka has told of skiing trips with the family where her father would hold her back with his ski stick attached to the back of her suit while also propelling himself ahead to win because the competitive spirits in the family were so high. Ivanka loves it though, and she's not ashamed of that fact. She knows that the competitive spirit and drive is what brought her to where she is today. Without that, she certainly wouldn't be the woman we all know.

To give a little bit of backstory, Ivanka Marie was born October 30, 1981, in Manhattan, New York and grew up there. Her mother, Ivana, is of Czechoslovakian descent and is proud of it. In fact, Ivana made her children learn French and have a good handle on the Czech language. Ivanka's father, Donald Trump, is of German and Scottish descent. He is the household name that has helped Ivanka springboard into her career. You can tell by the traits of her parents that she would grow up to be a go-getter. One of the best stories I can think of to describe this point is how Ivanka would go out of her way to see her dad after her parents divorced when she was 10. She lived with her mother and brothers in the same building as her father, but on different floors. She would stop by on her way to school every morning and go see him at work everyday on her way home. Ivanka has told stories of how she would sit in her father's office and listen to him make deals over the phone. It has been said that brothers Don Jr. and Eric didn't have the "clearance" that Ivanka did with Donald. If she called the office, it went straight to him, no matter what time it was or how busy he might have been. During recesses, she would hide in the janitor's closet at school simply to call him. Ivanka has always loved the world of business, and she tied that love to the love of her father and has done all she can to blossom in that. She went out of her way to learn all about the business world and how her father sees it so she can copy that model and make it work for herself.

Growing up in the spotlight wasn't easy for Ivanka. While her parents were in the middle of their divorce, there was a scandal that happened with her father and Marla Maples. On more than one occasion, the paparazzi would chase young Ivanka home (she was only 9 at the time) asking her what she thought about what her dad had said. Later, she said that out of that, she learned to put her guard up and keep it up, because that's not something she wants to have happen to her again emotionally.

For schooling, she went to Chapin School until she was 15, and then her parents decided to send her to Choate Rosemary Hall in Connecticut. Ever the adventurous spirit, she hated the boarding school life so much that she decided to do something else interesting on the side. At this point, when most people feel like they're in prison or missing out on the fun their friends are having, like Ivanka claimed, they would simply find a hobby like reading or collecting bugs (she had two brothers, anything is possible). Not Ivanka though; she wanted real adventure, so she became a model. The thing about reading and collecting bugs is that you don't get paid to do them. Ivanka had to pay for her own phone bill and therefore needed some extra money on the side. Modelling was the avenue through which she decided to work. In the short run (and ultimately the long run), it worked well for her. She modeled for Versace and Thierry Mugler as well as doing an ad campaign for Tommy Hilfiger. She even ended up on the cover of *Seventeen* magazine, and in 1997 that was no small feat, even for a Trump! Since she also got to travel, it gave her most of the freedom and adventure she wanted. Her parents disapproved of her modelling career at first, because they feared she was too young to be in that industry. You could tell that eventually Donald was simply proud of his daughter and would proclaim how beautiful she was during interviews… even to the point of causing some controversy by saying that he would date her if she wasn't his daughter. Ivanka didn't let any of that hold her back though. She continued to model, at least up through 2004.

Most women at this point would be fine to simply stay with what was working. Ivanka never had any intention of staying on as a model; it was simply a means to an end for her. After graduating from high school, she went on to Georgetown University for two years before transferring to Wharton Business School at the University of Pennsylvania. She graduated summa cum laude with a bachelor's degree. So not only did she get her bachelor's degree while still modelling, she got a 4.0 GPA and graduated with honors. If that doesn't show you who Ivanka Trump is, then nothing after this point will convince you. Ivanka knew what she wanted out of life, and she wasn't about to let anyone get in her way. She recalled a moment where she was sitting in a friend's apartment looking out over the New York City skyline and realized something was missing. In her mind, that something was a building with her name on it. Much like her father, she has a goal in mind, but I believe in some ways, she will go even farther than Donald ever went… and she will do it all as a woman.

Ivanka is breaking all the rules when it comes to women in the workplace. For a year, she tried to separate herself from the family name by working with another developing firm, but realized that there is nothing to be ashamed of as a Trump and came back home to work with her family. After 5 years of working for the Trump Organization, she was made executive vice president of development and acquisition along with her brothers Don Jr. and Eric. Her main tasks included expanding Trump Hotel brand, helping with the interior design of the hotels, and overseeing the real estate brokerage internationally. She did it all well and she loved every second of it. She has helped grow the Trump name to be more than just about real estate. To the world, the name "Trump" means "business" and "success". Much of that is thanks to Ivanka. She has marketed not only her father's company, but her own line of products as well. Thanks to social media it has become easier to get the word out more quickly and Ivanka uses that to her and her family's advantage.

I mentioned some of the products that Ivanka has produced at the beginning, but we can't focus on Ivanka being an entrepreneur without mentioning that Donald has also done some of the same things himself. I wouldn't be surprised if she got the idea from her father at some point, since they spent so much time together while she was growing up. Ivanka did it a bit more effectively, but she has also been able to self-promote because she can model for her own merchandise, as she has for Trump Organization at some points in the past. It first started with Ivanka Trump Fine Jewelry, which started after a diamond-district merchant approached her about some real estate. They made an exchange, where she lends her name to his company, and since that time Ivanka has made a name for her lifestyle brand. Ivanka Trump clothing, shoes, sunglasses and handbags were sold at Nordstrom and Dillard's. They sold well until there was controversy over Ivanka Trump becoming a part of her father's presidential campaign and the scandal that came with remarks Mr. Trump made in 1998 regarding women. Nordstrom dropped her clothing line entirely, sales dropped drastically overall, and many people boycotted her clothing line and any store that still sold it. Ivanka has not let that phase her as she has continued to work with her father. She has stated multiple times in the past that she knows who her father really is, and people would do well not to hold past mistakes against him.

Ivanka is no stranger to the dating game; she has had her share of hits and misses. During college she dated Greg Hersch, an investment banker that worked for different companies like Salomon Brothers, Bear Stearns, and UBS. They were together for almost 4 years while Ivanka was in college. Then from 2001 to 2005, she dated a man by the name of James "Bingo" Gubelmann, who was a socialite, documentary producer, and playboy. She finally found true love with Jared Kushner, a Modern Orthodox Jew, real estate developer, and owner of the

New York *Observer*. They had been set up on business lunch with a real estate broker in 2005 who thought they would work well together. They dated for almost 3 years, only to break up in 2008 because Jared's parents didn't approve of Ivanka since she didn't share the same faith. Jared and Ivanka do end up getting married in 2009 after Ivanka converted to Judaism. Having Presbyterian roots, it may seem strange for that to matter, but to a hardcore Jewish family, who you marry is everything. We can safely conclude that she loves Jared enough to convert for him. She studied under a rabbi for a year before converting because she was that serious, and that's what it takes to convert to Modern Orthodox Judaism. They had a very lavish Jewish ceremony. Ivanka and Jared now have three beautiful children; Arabella, Joseph, and Theodore.

For Ivanka, converting to Judaism was a big deal, not because it was a big change, but because she felt it was the right change. Judaism is a big part of her life and how she and her family interact together. Ivanka and Jared send their children to

Jewish schools and are raising their children in the ways of Judaism. Hearing what the children are learning confirms to them as parents that what they are doing is the right thing. Being Jewish is something that they do together as a family. Ivanka's father, Donald, says it was a surprise that she converted to Judaism, but he's happy for her. Ivanka has been involved in a lot of different Jewish charities since that time. After she converted the Trump's support of anything Jewish went up significantly, if it hadn't already been there before. United Hatzalah and Chai Lifeline are a few charities that she has helped and given donations to in the past. Chai Lifeline is a New York City based nonprofit, volunteer organization that primarily works with children battling cancer, while United Hatzalah is a Jerusalem-based nonprofit EMS organization. Ivanka's father and younger brother Eric have both given sizable contributions to United Hatzalah in the past as well. Ivanka is also a strong supporter of Israel and maintaining good relations with them.

Until politics entered the picture, much of Ivanka's recent life has been on-screen, as she has helped her father with his shows The Apprentice and The Celebrity Apprentice. These have taken up the majority of her time, since she was on both of them from 2006 until her father announced that he would be running for president. She knew that doing these shows came with the territory of working for her father and has done well to defend him in situations where the media have tried to smear him. She knows his heart and his character and will assure you that who you see on TV is the real Donald Trump, and he is not faking any of it. He really is a kind man with a big heart for people. Ivanka is the example of a daughter that truly loves her father, and she's always known that he loves her. Many people may not realize this, but Ivanka and Donald don't do these shows because they have so much free time on their hands. They do these shows to build the brand that is Trump. If it wasn't for The Apprentice and The Celebrity Apprentice, would you really know who Donald Trump was? Would you know who Ivanka Trump was? I know I wouldn't (admittedly I didn't know who the latter REALLY was until recently). Ivanka is always in the business of marketing and advertising, and she knows what she wants and she knows what the public wants. She also knows how to make money getting what the public wants to them.

Some of the other shows Ivanka has been on are not so obvious however, unless you watch a lot of reality TV. She was the host of the Miss Teen USA Pageant in 1997 (partially owned by her father, Donald), and she was also a guest judge on *Project Runway Season 3*. Ivanka and her husband, Jared, were also in season 4 episode 6 of *Gossip Girl*, where they briefly portrayed themselves.

Ivanka has also been a champion of women in the workplace. As I've mentioned, I knew next to nothing about Ivanka Trump, only that she was somehow related to Donald. However, as I've learned more about her, I do believe that she has helped break down the barriers that have held women in the workplace back by plowing through and establishing herself. She has not only done so as a woman in the workplace, but also a mother who knows the limits and has learned to juggle both work and home life. Through her own life, she has shown that it is not impossible to have a job and have children… especially happy and healthy children. She has admitted that there was a time when she got discouraged because she thought she wasn't doing something right. The societal pressure to do either work or have a family were strong, but she finally came to a place where she realized it wasn't about doing one or the other, but learning how to enjoy and cherish each moment. That doesn't simply apply to family, though she has said that is where she uses it the most. Living in the moment is how you get more accomplished in life; look forward to the future and make plans, but live in the now and enjoy every moment with your loved ones.

Ivanka is showing the world how to live in each moment and treasure the time we have, not just with family, but also in the business world. She is a firm believer in longer maternity leave for women and that their jobs should be there for them when they return. This is a big hot-button topic in America in recent years as many are finding out the maternity leave times of other countries in comparison. As a working mother, Ivanka believes that women should be respected and given equal pay and workload. She has certainly proven that she can do it, and she knows that there are many women that can do it too. She is simply trying to make it easier for all women now and the generations to come. She has written two books, both of which talk about working. The first one is titled *The Trump Card: Playing to Win in Work and Life.* The second one is called *Women Who Work: Rewriting the Rules for Success,* and it came out of the movement by the same name that Ivanka started in 2014. This movement is based on the idea that there are women who can be in business and have families. Real women who have started businesses and are driven, like Ivanka. Women who have become successful, and still choose to have families. They have learned to have the best of both worlds and continue to live in the moment. Ivanka has used social media to really promote this idea and it has been widely accepted by the public. Many critics, however, have spoken out about the book and its lack of using real-life women as examples of women who work.

Through Ivanka's example, women are becoming inspired to try new things. For example, since Donald Trump announced his intent to run for president, Ivanka has been more involved in politics. It started off small, but once she introduced her father at the Republican National Convention, everyone knew she was in it for the long haul. Many people see it as almost hypocritical that the Trump's have been one way for so long and seemingly changed their minds on many political things, but it's always been about one thing: winning. Since the very start of Ivanka's life (and even before she was born), the Trump family has focused on that one aspect. Who is on the winning team? Can we make the winning team win faster and harder? How much money should we invest in the winning team? Therefore, when Donald Trump made the decision to run for president, all of the Trump's got on board. Ivanka became something of a spokesperson for her father, smoothing the ruffled feathers of some and shaking the dry ground of others. Ivanka has helped her father rebuild the Trump name to mean more than "business." Now it also stands for "politics". It has become less about what they do and more about who they are. Since her father became president, they are now officially politicians... and they are even redefining what it is to be a politician.

During the RNC, Ivanka made it clear that she is a millennial who is not set on simply being a Republican or Democrat. She proved that with her own life by giving to different party candidates over the last decade. In 2007, she donated money to Hillary Clinton's campaign; in 2012, she supported Mitt Romney for president; and in 2013, Ivanka and her husband helped raise $40,000 for Cory Booker's U.S. Senate campaign. As someone with this mindset, and a businessman for a president, she is helping shape what the future of politics will look like in this country. I believe that even the mainstream media as we know it will change with Donald Trump as president. Much of it will be for the best. Ivanka's husband, Jared, has become an integral part of the Trump campaign and family as he has now been named one of the senior advisors to the president, while Ivanka has been named President Trump's assistant. They even moved to Washington, D.C., in January of 2017. When the Trump's do things, they do it as a family. Many families would do well to learn from this model. There are times to talk business and there are times to let it go, the wisdom comes in knowing when these times are and not pushing it too much. There is a story about the Trump Organization that says the higher you go in the company, the harder it is to find the line between what would be considered family and what would be considered business. To the Trump's however, family is business, and business is family. I believe they've carried much of this same mentality with them into the White House and will use it to run this country effectively.

There are many people who still find things to complain about with Ivanka Trump. For instance, after her speech at the

Republican National Convention, her clothing line sent out a tweet mentioning the dress and where to buy it. Many people saw this as a monetization scheme. Although it is a way to make money and it's wonderful marketing, doesn't the media usually do that with any nice pieces we see? If you flip through any tabloid you'll see them all talking about what a celebrity wore to what event and where to buy one if one so desires. For Ivanka this instance happened twice, and the second time was after a *60 Minutes* family interview in which she wore a stunning bracelet and the next morning her company sent out an email blast promoting said bracelet. Much of the chatter that has come at Ivanka's expense has been fairly idle and childish at times. She simply lets it roll off her back as she continues onward toward whatever it is that she is accomplishing in the moment. If anyone would know, it would be the Trump's that controversy breeds attention, which in turn breeds business. It was only because of the amount of attention that Donald Trump got and the waves that he made that he became president. Ivanka made sure that he not only received attention, but that he received the right attention. She made sure the the Trump political brand was exactly what it needed to be, and her husband Jared (who has a rather lucrative real estate business himself) has made sure that the brand continues to grow and get the good coverage that it needs.

A lingering question in everyone's mind is how Ivanka's friendship with Chelsea Clinton has affected her. As of March 2016, they hadn't really been seen together in public because of the fact that their parents had run against each other in the 2016 presidential election. Chelsea has said that her parents raised her to believe that friendships are more important than politics, but it seems that family comes before friendships for both women. During the election time and especially at the Republican National Convention, many conjectured that Ivanka's policy goals sounded more like Hillary Clinton's than her own father's, and almost blamed Ivanka's relationship with Chelsea on that. Although the two didn't see each other a lot, I'm not sure how many more times they will actually meet in public because of how Ivanka's position in the nation has changed.

Aside from Ivanka's friendship with Chelsea, one of the major issues is what her role in the White House is. Currently her title is assistant to the president, though it is an unpaid government position. Although she has taken on many of the tasks and responsibilities of the First Lady, she denies any allegations that she has taken on the role. Melania has been staying in New York City with President Trump's youngest son, Barron, while he finishes school. Ivanka has become a part of the president's inner circle, but it would only make sense since she also helped him run one of the biggest organizations in the world for a minimum of 5 years, if not more. However in the minds of many, a woman who is officially an unpaid government employee should not be able to see many of the classified things that the president can see, whether she's considered part of the inner circle of the president or not.

Ivanka has done all she can to comply with any of the ethical problems that the media and naysayers have brought up, just as her father had to. Because Donald and Ivanka are now government employees it creates a conflict of interest to have their faces associated with any one company. They now represent the people as a whole and not just one aspect of the people. The Trump website has removed all or nearly all of the pictures and sayings of and by Donald and Ivanka, as they have been making as much of a break from the Trump Organization as possible. It has proven a little more difficult for Ivanka to completely make all breaks from the business world since she still owns her own clothing and lifestyle business. All of the backlash she received in 2016 regarding her clothing line has only helped to propel sales, especially in China, where her company has gained provisional rights for three trademarks, giving it something of a monopoly there. In other countries there have been trademark agreements. Countries like Puerto Rico, Canada, the U.S., and the Philippines. This has caused many people to wonder if she and her husband are the right people to be advisors to the President of the United States. This would generally be frowned upon because it's hard to be unbiased if you have connections to something in the world like a business. It has the potential to create a conflict of interest when consulting the president on certain matters. However, Ivanka has done what she can by moving the business's assets to a family-run trust fund that will help determine if any of the potential business ventures will cause a conflict of interest. Rarely has anything stopped Ivanka from doing what she wanted, so if she feels that helping her father with the presidency is more important, she will put the business aside for the family she loves.

From this brief biography we can see that Ivanka Trump is a woman who is driven, passionate, and caring. Unlike other women, Ivanka has done well to keep herself out of any unnecessary news and tabloids. Call me naive, but if I hadn't heard of Ivanka Trump until around election time, then the chances are she wasn't causing enough waves for me to hear about her. That is the sign of a good person: one who keeps themselves out of the news for as long as possible. She loves her family and will do anything for them. She has followed in her father's footsteps (enough that many believe she will be the one to take over Trump Organization when the time comes), and has taken what she's learned to a whole new level. Ivanka Trump has learned how to balance her work and private life and how to show love to her children in the best ways. She has found a faith that she believes in, takes it very seriously, and guides her family to do the same. She makes friends with people that many would find unusual and she has proven that politics is not what it used to be by supporting the side that she agrees with the most, instead of the one affiliated with whatever party she's put herself in.

What else could I say about Ivanka Trump that hasn't already been said? She knows how to project herself to get what she wants, she will help people that need it, and she pushes for justice in any situation. In short, Ivanka Trump is the woman that all women should follow as an example in that she has blazed a trail for us all to follow and doesn't care what others think of her. When she starts something, she's sure to finish it. She can be trusted to handle confidential matters with the greatest ease, and makes even the worst situations look manageable. Ivanka Trump is the woman we need by Donald Trump's side helping to run the country as she continues to show what it looks like to be a woman who works, as well as a woman who takes family very seriously.

Made in the USA
Las Vegas, NV
13 June 2021